Baby Brother Wonders

Gitanjali Rao

Copyright © 2015 Gitanjali Rao.

All rights reserved. No part of this book may be used or reproduced by any means, graphic, electronic, or mechanical, including photocopying, recording, taping or by any information storage retrieval system without the written permission of the publisher except in the case of brief quotations embodied in critical articles and reviews.

LifeRich Publishing is a registered trademark of The Reader's Digest Association, Inc.

LifeRich Publishing books may be ordered through booksellers or by contacting:

LifeRich Publishing
1663 Liberty Drive
Bloomington, IN 47403
www.liferichpublishing.com
1 (888) 238-8637

Because of the dynamic nature of the Internet, any web addresses or links contained in this book may have changed since publication and may no longer be valid. The views expressed in this work are solely those of the author and do not necessarily reflect the views of the publisher, and the publisher hereby disclaims any responsibility for them.

Any people depicted in stock imagery provided by Thinkstock are models, and such images are being used for illustrative purposes only. Certain stock imagery © Thinkstock.

ISBN: 978-1-4897-0408-5 (sc)
ISBN: 978-1-4897-0407-8 (e)

Printed in the United States of America.

LifeRich Publishing rev. date: 02/12/2015

I dedicate this book to my baby brother who fills our life with joy every day.

If I peeped in to my baby brother's mind
and wandered in to his wonderland,
I would wonder why my pacifier flies high up in the air?
When I'm in my garden, and I laugh without a care.

I would wonder why my airplane bounces back to me?
While the one in the sky, flies smoothly.

I would wonder why my parents want me
to greet strangers every day?
Sometimes they scare me, and I want to run away!

I would wonder why my sister sees
a spider and really freaks?
While I can feast on it, for days and weeks!!

I would wonder why my family does not
understand what I say?
Even though I communicate, "See, I want to play!!"

I would wonder why the sun is in my sister's cup?
And I always see it, high up!!

CPSIA information can be obtained
at www.ICGtesting.com
Printed in the USA
BVHW020155040319
541693BV00022B/337/P